Other books in the series:

Prophet Muhammad ﷺ

Abu Bakr as-Siddiq رضي الله عنه

Umar ibn al-Khattab رضي الله عنه

Uthman ibn Affan رضي الله عنه

Hasan and Husayn İbn Ali رضي الله عنه

Khadija bint Khuwaylid رضي الله عنها

Aisha bint Abu Bakr رضي الله عنها

Fatima رضي الله عنها bint Muhammad ﷺ

THE AGE OF BLISS

KHALID ﷺ
IBN AL-WALID

ÖMER YILMAZ

NEW JERSEY • LONDON • FRANKFURT • CAIRO • JAKARTA

TUGHRA
BOOKS

New Jersey

Copyright © 2017 by Tughra Books

20 19 18 17   2 3 4

All rights reserved. No part of this book may be reproduced or transmitted in any form or by any means, electronic or mechanical, including photocopying, recording or by any information storage and retrieval system without permission in writing from the Publisher.

Translated by Ebru Kösedağ
Edited by Clare Duman

Published by Tughra Books
335 Clifton Ave., Clifton,
NJ, 07011, USA

www.tughrabooks.com

Library of Congress Cataloging-in-Publication Data Available

ISBN: 978-1-59784-379-9

TABLE OF CONTENTS

Khalid ibn al-Walid رضي الله عنه

His Childhood

Among the children playing games in the streets of Mecca were two brothers whose family had a military background. They were playing soldiers. Hisham made bows and arrows from branches he had collected, while Khalid played the role of commander.

The children's mother, Lubaba, was a caring person who attached great importance to their education, while their father, Walid, was well-known as a commander of the army in Mecca. So, with military service being second nature to him, Khalid grew up from a young age a competent horse rider and eager to learn to throw a spear while on horseback.

Khalid enjoyed sports, which made him physically strong, and he triumphed in wrestling matches he took part in at fairs. On one occasion, he wrestled with Umar ibn al-Khattab, may Allah be pleased with him, and beat him, leaving him with a broken leg. As well as being physically strong, Khalid also had inner strength, displaying important qualities such as courage, heroism and generosity, all of which were much admired by Arabs. So Khalid attracted attention and was entrusted with the post of administrator of the dragon cavalry, which led him eventually to great fame and achievement as a commander in the army.

A Lesson Learned from His Brother

One very hot day, Khalid and his brother, Hisham, were walking slowly through the streets of Medina, waiting for the temperature to drop. Most people wouldn't venture out in such heat, but the brothers had good reason to on that day. Their brother, Walid, had been taken prisoner by the Muslims at the Battle of Badr, so they had come to Medina to rescue him from captivity. Hisham spoke, breaking the silence:

"Had you been taken prisoner, you could have saved yourself from captivity as the Muslims would release prisoners in return for teaching them to read and write." Khalid replied: "Yes, I was surprised to hear that."

Khalid learned to read and write during his trips to Syria, Egypt, and Yemen, with the trade caravans.

Since, at that time, few people could read or write, Prophet Muhammad, peace and blessings be upon him, offered anyone captured at the Battle of Badr their freedom, if they taught ten Muslims to read and write. Khalid was astonished to learn how greatly valued the skills of reading and writing were in Islam. He realized he knew nothing about Islam and wondered what kind of religion this was. He was just trying to find a way to free his brother. Had he known Islam's first command was 'Read!' he would have understood. As Khalid's brother, Walid, could neither read nor write he could only gain his freedom by his brothers paying a ransom for him, which they did.

The three brothers set off for Mecca, but Walid's mind was still in Medina, pondering what good treatment the Muslims had afforded him and how deeply impressed he had been. It was for this reason that he wanted to know more about the noble Prophet and Islam. However, he didn't know how to tell his brothers what was on his mind, but he tried to explain. Khalid said to him: "You sound as though you're praising the religion of Islam. Didn't you come to Badr to fight against the Muslims?"

Walid thought for a moment. He realized that, at first, it was true, he had been against Islam, and felt so much hatred for Muslims that he had come to Badr to fight against them. But later he had realized that they were not as bad as he had thought. During his imprisonment in Medina, they had treated him more as a friend than a prisoner. They had shared their food and drink with him, and had explained to him that both their religion and their Prophet demanded such behavior.

The noble Prophet's uncle, Abbas, may Allah be pleased with him, had also been a prisoner and, out of respect for him, the blessed Prophet's friends had wanted to untie his hands. But the Messenger of Allah believed in treating everyone the same, so he had insisted that all prisoners should have their hands untied.

As Walid recalled that event, he paused to consider for a moment, and then realized he could admit to feeling a deep love for the Messenger of Allah and for Islam. He also wanted to experience the same feeling of brotherhood which he saw in Muslim people.

Without another thought, all of a sudden, he told Khalid and Hisham that he wanted to turn back. He expected them to accept his decision with respect, but it was as though his words had stabbed them in the back.

Khalid thought he had misheard his brother but, having questioned him further, he realized that Walid had, or was about to, become a Muslim. He reacted badly to what he considered was an intolerable situation. Shocked by his brothers' violent reaction, Walid slipped away and returned to Medina. Khalid and Hisham at once gave chase, took him back to Mecca and imprisoned him.

Walid's heart was full of love for the blessed Prophet, and he wanted only to be with the Messenger of Allah, so somehow he escaped from the prison and returned to Medina.

Khalid and the Battle of Uhud

*I*t was March 625 and the Meccans, still smarting from their defeat at the hands of the Muslims, gathered an army of nearly three thousand soldiers to do battle with them again. As the Meccans trusted their own military capacity, they gave the command of the cavalry of the army of Mecca to Khalid. Khalid gathered his army early and set up military quarters in the foothills of Mount Uhud; first, to survey the battlefield and, secondly, to inspect his soldiers. During his reconnaissance, Khalid noticed a pass where a group of fifty Muslim archers, under the command of Abdullah ibn Jubayr, may Allah be pleased with him, were waiting under cover. The pass was strategically critical for the out-come of the war, and the noble Prophet charged Abdullah with the command that: "no enemy caval-ry shall penetrate through that pass." So the Messen-ger of Allah ordered his soldier: "Win or lose, do not leave your position until further notice."

During the battle, Khalid, like a hunter, kept his eyes fixed on those soldiers positioned in the pass. He remained at his post as though it were he the blessed Prophet had been addressing.

When the battle started, Muslim soldiers were attacking the Meccan soldiers as if they were run-ning through the gardens of Paradise, and they were very successful. As the army of Islam proceeded to the enemy headquarters, Mecca's soldiers fled from the area without a backward glance. Abdullah ibn Jubayr did his best to persuade the archers to main-tain their positions, but to no avail. Only ten remained with him.

When Khalid saw that the archers had fled, he saw his opportunity. He and his men advanced through the pass left undefended by the archers, and besieged the Muslim soldiers from behind, kill-ing seventy of them, including Hamza ibn Abdul

Muttalib, may Allah be pleased with him, the noble Prophet's uncle and milk sibling.

The Messenger of Allah, deeply upset by the martyrdom of Hamza, wept and commanded: "No one has ever had such misfortune as you. This is the most terrible news for me. O the uncle of the Messenger of Allah! O Allah's lion, Hamza! May Allah have mercy on you. I know very well that you always looked after the interests of your family and did good deeds. If mourning were possible, I would mourn for you."

There were no winners or losers at the Battle of Uhud, but one thing was never forgotten: the military genius of Khalid.

Khalid and the Battle of the Trench

The Meccans, with a large army of ten thousand soldiers, came to Medina to do battle with the Muslims. The blessed Prophet, who liked to consult with others before making a decision, agreed with his Companions—they would fight a defensive battle. One of the Companions, Salman, may Allah be pleased with him, from Persia, made an interesting observation. In Persia, if a city was vulnerable to attack from the outside, it would be surrounded with deep trenches. Salman said it would be useful to dig such trenches around Medina, and the blessed Prophet agreed. It was the first time Khalid had seen such trenches. Although he had grown up like a soldier since his childhood, he had never seen such a defense tactic before. The Meccans were forced to turn back, as they were unable to cross the trenches.

The Peace Treaty of Hudaybiya

The Messenger of Allah had a dream in which he was visiting the Ka'ba. Having been born and brought up in Mecca, he was especially fond of the Ka'ba but, after living in Medina for the past six years, he profoundly missed this special place, and this dream was evidence of that. So he asked a friend to arrange a visit to the Ka'ba, and all the Muslims in Medina were happy to join in with the preparations.

The noble Prophet's sole purpose for traveling to Mecca was to visit the Ka'ba so, to show his peaceful intent, he took with him seventy sacrificial camels. However, as soon as the Meccans heard that the noble Prophet was approaching the city, they sent Khalid and his cavalry to the hill called Ghamim, to prevent him from entering. Khalid watched the blessed Prophet and his Companions from a distance as they prayed, shoulder to shoulder, and he was impressed by them and, for some reason, felt affection towards the beloved Prophet.

Khalid's soldiers were expecting the order to attack, but Khalid told them he had delayed plans to attack the Muslims. As a result of both sides holding back, the Peace Treaty of Hudaybiya was agreed between the Muslims and the polytheists, whereupon the noble Prophet and his Companions returned home without visiting Ka'ba on this occasion.

Khalid Becomes a Muslim

When Prophet Muhammad, peace and blessings be upon him, began his Prophethood, Khalid ibn al-Walid was not only a polytheist, he also sought to fight the noble Prophet at every opportunity. In fact, so strong was his antipathy towards the blessed Prophet that when the latter arrived in Mecca to perform the minor pilgrimage (*Umrah*), Khalid left the city, so as not to encounter him. But the noble Prophet was merciful and, despite Khalid's actions, he wanted to show kindness towards him. Khalid's brother, Walid, may Allah be pleased with him, was already a follower of the blessed Prophet, and when they arrived in Mecca he wrote a letter to his brother, Khalid, which stated: "I really don't understand why you resist Islam. How strange that a person like you does not accept Islam! Recently, the noble Prophet asked me where you were, and I told him that Allah will bring him to us. The Messenger of Allah then said to me: "How strange that a person like Khalid does not accept Islam! I wish he would direct his heroism against polytheists, and not only against Muslims. It would be better for him, and for us, if he were to be on our side." My brother! You've missed so many good opportunities at different times. Don't miss this opportunity that awaits you now."

Khalid was thrilled with his brother's letter, and the noble Prophet's words of praise made him very happy. Even before receiving the letter, Khalid was reluctant to fight against the Messenger of Allah because he felt he was on the wrong side in the battlefield. He began thinking this way because, as cavalry commander of polytheists when the blessed Prophet had arrived at Hudaybiya, Khalid had taken aim at the Messenger of Allah who, even though he knew his situation, fearlessly continued to lead the Noon Prayer for his followers. Because the Muslims were not defending themselves, Khalid decided to delay his attack until the Afternoon Prayer. This time the noble Prophet put half his congregation on guard, while the remainder prayed. On seeing this, Khalid ibn al-Walid was shocked to realize that the Muslims appeared to have Divine protection. This shook his confidence and he muttered to himself: "What should I do?" He knew he was doing the wrong thing, but he didn't know how to put things right.

Another day, when he was feeling dispirited, he had a dream. In his dream, he was hemmed into a tight place, thirsty and sweating with anxiety. He was confused when suddenly that narrow, waterless place turned into a huge green area with the pleasant sound of flowing water. Waking up, he realized his dream was a sign of what he wanted to do. Now his mind was made up—he would go and visit the blessed Prophet and shout out to the universe that he believed in Allah!

But before that, he needed to find a companion, and when he explained his wishes to Uthman ibn Talha, his friend immediately agreed to go with him. They met up and set out at dawn, meeting Amr ibn

As on the way who, having the same purpose in mind, joined them.

The Messenger of Allah, upon hearing that three important people were on their way to see him, was very happy and said to one of his Companions: "Mecca sent you its beloved ones."

In preparation for meeting the noble Prophet face to face, Khalid ibn al-Walid put on his most beautiful robe and was waiting when his brother, Walid, arrived and said: "Come on, hurry up. The Messenger of Allah is expecting you and is very pleased to receive you."

As he approached the door which would take him into the presence of the blessed Prophet, he was at once feeling excited to meet him face to face, but also guilty for the many years he had spent fighting the Muslims and even killing many of them at the Battle of Uhud. How could he face the gaze of the Messenger of Allah? His heart was racing and his whole body was breaking out into a sweat. As soon as he opened the door, he smelled the unique fragrance of the noble Prophet. Now he was in the presence of the Messenger of Allah. He saluted nervously. The Messenger of Allah accepted his salute with a smile and showed him to his place. Then Khalid recited the Testimony of Faith (*kalima sha-hadah*), and became noble Khalid ibn al-Walid, may Allah be pleased with him.

Upon Khalid's becoming Muslim, the Messenger of Allah said, "I thank Allah who gave you guidance. I knew that one day you would be blessed." Khalid was so pleased with the noble Prophet's words that he became even more embarrassed, and asked the blessed Prophet: "O Messenger of Allah! I have fought against you in wars. Please pray for my absolution." Then the beloved Prophet replied: "Islam erases past sins." Although reassured by these words, Khalid still wanted the noble Prophet to pray for his forgiveness and he pleaded: "O Messenger of Allah, please pray for me, that by becoming Muslim my previous sins are forgiven." Then the blessed Prophet prayed: "O my Lord! Forgive Khalid's previous sins." After Khalid ibn al-Walid's conversion to Islam, his fellow travelers Amr ibn As and Usman ibn Talha, may Allah be pleased with them, came into the presence of the blessed Prophet and also became Muslims.

Side by Side with the Noble Prophet

After becoming Muslim, Khalid ibn al-Walid, thanks to his literate background, became clerk to the noble Prophet, and occupied a house very close to him. He was also at the blessed Prophet's side during the farewell pilgrimage, when the beloved Prophet addressed his friends in the words of the Farewell Sermon. In this sermon, he laid down a roadmap for future generations until the Day of Judgment. Then he offered a sacrifice and shaved his head. This particular ritual during the pilgrimage was common to everyone, but this time with one difference. As the Messenger of Allah was being shaved, people, including Khalid, gathered to take a lock of his sacred hair. As the noble Prophet's fringe was cut, Khalid asked: "O Allah's Messenger! May I have a lock of your hair?" The Messenger of Allah did not refuse him, but sent him on his way with a lock of his hair. Khalid held the hair to his face and kissed it. From then on, he kept the lock of hair in his turban to remember the blessed Prophet by. When Khalid was victorious in battle, he believed it was the lock of hair which brought him good luck. After all, that hair was a piece of the noble Prophet, and Allah would never see him defeated.

During the Battle of Yarmuk, Khalid's turban fell to the ground and he stopped fighting to search for it. People were amazed. What was the importance of a turban on the battlefield? It may have been an ordinary turban, but it contained the blessed Prophet's lock of hair. Therefore, this turban was more valuable to him than anything else, even his own life.

Khalid and the Battle of Muta

halid spent his days learning the basic principles of his new religion and, in addition and importantly, he wrote down the details of his conversion. The non-believers in Mecca were deeply upset by Khalid's choice of Islam, and even more despairing when other commanders decided to become Muslims.

Meanwhile, the Messenger of Allah was sending out letters to the rulers of neighboring states, inviting them to embrace Islam. One such letter was sent to the governor of Damascus, who ordered that the envoy who brought the letter should be killed. This caused a huge scandal at the time, and is still remembered today.

The Messenger of Allah, who was deeply upset by this murder, broke the bad news to his people. He then sent, as a last resort, a delegation to the governor, who promptly murdered another fifteen of their number. This was the final straw for the noble Prophet, and he felt compelled to send a military expedition to march on Muta. Three thousand armed Muslim soldiers, Khalid ibn al-Walid among them, set up military camp. That was the first time Khalid engaged battle as a Muslim. After performing the Noon Prayer, the noble Prophet said: "Zayd ibn Haritha will be the commander of the defending army. If he is killed, Jafar ibn Abi Talib will take over as commander. If he is also killed, Abdullah ibn Rawaha will take his place. If he too is killed, then the Muslim soldiers will make their own choice of commander."

After the blessed Prophet had given his orders, one of the Jews said to Zayd, may Allah be pleased with him: "Say goodbye to your family and, indeed, write your last will. Even should the noble Prophet choose a hundred people as commander, they all will surely die. If the Messenger of Allah asks you to be commander, it means you will not be coming back." Then Zayd replied: "I proclaim that the Prophet belongs to Allah."

Before the army set off, the blessed Prophet gave Zayd a white flag and ordered him to invite people to embrace Islam wherever he went. Then he said to all his soldiers: "Follow Allah's orders, do nothing illegal, treat people well." In addition, he ordered his soldiers not to hurt children, worshippers, women or the elderly. The Messenger of Allah never wanted children to suffer, even in times of war. He also commanded that no trees should be damaged or buildings set on fire. As the army moved off, people bade them farewell them with the words: "May Allah protect you from danger."

When the governor of Damascus heard that the army of Islam was coming towards them, he requested help from the Byzantine Emperor. Together with these back-up troops, he mustered an army of one hundred thousand soldiers. When the Muslim army received this information regarding the Greek troops, they agreed that the noble Prophet should be made aware of the situation. One of the potential commanders was Abdullah ibn Rawaha, may Allah be pleased with him, an effective orator and poet. The Messenger of Allah had once said of him: "His poems strike the hearts of polytheists better than arrows."

Abdullah ibn Rawaha rallied the people around him with the words: "We are fighting a battle, not with the strength of our weapons, but with the power of our religion. Let's go, let's fight. Ultimately, there will be one of two possible beautiful results: either victory or martyrdom."

Never before had Khalid seen an army of soldiers so completely outnumbered by the enemy, willing to engage in battle, emboldened by the strength of their faith. Every soldier, including Khalid, accepted Abdullah's words and agreed to continue fighting. Khalid began the war as a rank-and-file soldier, but ended it as commander.

The army of Islam stopped in the Muta region to prepare for battle against an army that was superior to them in all aspects. Commander Zayd led his troops into battle from the front, carrying in his hand the white flag the noble Prophet had given him. When he was martyred, his armor was riddled with spears. With Zayd dead, Jafar, may Allah be please with him, took control of the troops and carried the flag. He fought and advanced into the middle of the enemy troops. Suddenly he realized that his hand had been cut off and the flag had fallen, so he immediately took the flag in his other hand. Seriously injured by sword wounds, he still managed to place the flag under his arm when he lost his other hand. His troops hardly dared to take the flag from beneath their hero's arm, even when he lay dead. After brave Jafar had been martyred by losing both arms, the blessed Prophet said: "Allah has given him two wings in place of the two arms he lost, and with those Jafar flew to Paradise."

Abdullah ibn Rawaha took first the flag and then command of the army from Jafar and, gathering his soldiers, launched an attack on the enemy forces. When Abdullah, too, was felled by enemy spears, the Muslim soldiers were engaged in battle with the enemy troops. Each of the commanders appointed by the noble Prophet had been martyred and the army began to fall into disarray. At this point, Thabit ibn al-Arqam, may Allah be pleased with him, a veteran of the Battle of Badr, took the flag and delivered it to Khalid ibn al-Walid.

Khalid was a good man and much respected. He would never assume leadership of an army above a veteran of the Battle of Badr, but Thabit, who knew him well, insisted. Taking the flag, Khalid began to evaluate the situation. His men were outnumbered and exhausted, so he decided to change their positions. Those on the front line changed places with those at the back, and those on the left swapped with those on the right. These maneuvers panicked the enemy, as they assumed Muslim reinforcements had arrived. In the morning, Khalid ordered his troops into battle, fearlessly leading the attack and destroying nine swords as he fought. The Byzantine army was confused by the enemy's tactics, but actually Khalid's only concern was not so much to defeat the enemy, since to conquer an army of one hundred thousand with only three thousand was not possible, but to try and save the Islamic army from extinction. First, Khalid pulled back his troops from the right and the left, and then the central troops withdrew. The Byzantine army had no strength left to follow Khalid's soldiers.

Khalid ibn al-Walid:
The Sword of Allah

The Muslims of Medina noticed that the Messenger of Allah was particularly sad and asked him the reason. He gathered the people in the mosque and shared with them his deep sorrow at the martyrdom of the commanders in the Battle of Muta. He said: "My sorrow is because of the martyrs in the Battle of Muta. May Allah have mercy on their souls."

The Messenger of Allah appeared to be describing the battle as though he were actually there watching it. He described: "Our army was face to face with the enemy. First, Zayd ibn Haritha was martyred, then, Jafar ibn Abi Talib, taking the flag, rushed forward and fought bravely before he, too, was martyred. Beg forgiveness for your brothers. Later on, Abdullah ibn Rawaha took the flag and fought heroically before he, also, was slain, a martyr."

The Messenger of Allah was in tears as he described the unimaginable horror of events on the battlefield. He greatly valued those soldiers who had become martyrs for Islam. For example, his conversation with Jafar Tayyar, may Allah be pleased with him, on his return from Abyssinia, shows the depth of his respect for him. The noble Prophet was in Khaybar, which had just been conquered, when he embraced Jafar, kissed his forehead and said: "I don't know which makes me happier! Jafar's arrival or the conquest of Khaybar?"

But now, he had to tell people that Jafar had been martyred. Everyone could see the noble Prophet was in tears. After explaining what had happened in Muta, the blessed Prophet continued: "In the end, someone took one of the swords of Allah. O Allah, Khalid is also one of Your swords. May he and our army be triumphant." In this way, Khalid adopted the name *Sayfullah* which means the Sword of Allah. The first battle he fought as a Muslim was called 'the

War of the Commanders' Army', and gained Khalid great respect and admiration.

A few days later, Ya'la ibn Umayya, may Allah be pleased with him, arrived in Medina to inform the Messenger of Allah of the outcome of the battle of Muta. When the noble Prophet saw Ya'la, he said: "Let me explain before you start." Ya'la was surprised because the blessed Prophet had not been with them there, so how could he explain? His surprise was even greater as the noble Prophet started to describe every detail of the battle. When the blessed Prophet had finished speaking, Ya'la asked: "You have just described everything I was going to tell you. Would you mind if I asked how you did that?" The beloved Prophet explained: "Glorious Allah lifted the veil and I watched the battlefield."

As the soldiers were making the long journey home, the people of Medina could talk about nothing else. The blessed Prophet, accompanied by the Muslims in Medina, was on his way to meet the army. It was obvious from their appearance that the battle had been hard won, and Khalid was at the front, leading his men. The Messenger of Allah said to them,

"I can see you did not run away from the battle, but fought to the death."

When they heard the noble Prophet's words of praise, Khalid and all the returning soldiers were able to relax and rest easy. Khalid was alongside the blessed Prophet, who expressed his satisfaction at the success of the army and told him that from that moment on he would be known as *Sayfullah* meaning "Sword of Allah."

Khalid ibn al-Walid ﷺ

Khalid and the Conquest of Mecca

*I*t had been eight years since the Migration (*Hijra*) and, thanks to the Peace Treaty of Hudaybiya, Muslims and Meccans were living alongside each other peaceably. The Messenger of Allah was sitting in the mosque leading the Prayer when a group of people approached him. It was the same group which supported the noble Prophet against the Meccans in Hudaybiya, but now they needed help themselves. They told the Messenger of Allah that the Meccans had violated the Treaty of Hudaybiya, after only two years of peace, and attacked them. Twenty-three of their people had died in the attacks. Upon hearing this, the noble Prophet pledged to help those people.

The Messenger of Allah gave orders to his Companions to get ready to set off, but they were confused as to where they were going. The blessed Prophet wanted to enter Mecca without shedding blood, but in order to do that, he needed to surround Mecca with a strong army and force them to surrender. He sent news to the Muslims around Medina to get ready to move out and, once preparations had been completed, they were told that the destination was Mecca. An army of twelve thousand soldiers, including men from nearby tribes, set out from Medina. One of those soldiers was Khalid ibn al-Walid, whom the noble Prophet had appointed commander of the vanguard, and he began to move towards Mecca with his soldiers. Khalid felt they were being followed and when they caught the person who followed them, they discovered he was appointed as a spy to keep watch on the blessed Prophet. Obeying orders from the Messenger of Allah, Khalid first questioned him, and then arrested him.

At nightfall, the beloved Prophet ordered the army to stop and light fires. At first Khalid could not understand his plan. As more than ten thousand soldiers lit fires, the Meccans became alarmed and

asked their leader, Abu Sufyan, to check what was
going on. Khalid was on lookout with his soldiers
when he recognized Abu Sufyan coming towards
them. By making a fire, the noble Prophet enabled
the Meccans to see the size of the Muslim army.
They could see that he had the power to kill all of
them that night, without warning. But he didn't do
that, always preferring to win the enemy over instead
of destroying them. This fascinated Khalid, to see
how important it was to the blessed Prophet to win
the hearts of the people. In the morning, the Messenger of Allah divided the army into four. He appointed Khalid commander of the right side, meaning he
would enter Mecca from the south. When he arrived
on the lower side of the city, he saw that the Quraysh
had troops ready to fight. Khalid was warned not to
battle unless there was an attempt to fight, as the
blessed Prophet wanted to enter Mecca without shedding any blood. However, although he had no inten-
tion to fight the Meccans, he could not remain unre-
sponsive if they showed resistance. Before long, Khalid had defeated that small troop, and the remaining
soldiers threw down their swords to bring the fighting to an end. Khalid took out the flag he was given

by the Messenger of Allah and placed it near the houses. After that, he went to Safa, where the noble Prophet was waiting for him. Thus, the conquest of Mecca was complete. Allah's Messenger came close to the Ka'ba and performed the prostration of thankfulness. He saluted and kissed the Holy Black Stone.

As far as the Meccans were concerned, he was in a forgiving frame of mind, even though they once tortured him and even fought against him. Instead of taking his revenge against them, he responded with kindness. Khalid's respect towards the noble Prophet increased every day as he witnessed these events, and he always gave thanks to Allah for enabling the blessed Prophet to be victorious in the battle for Mecca. The Messenger of Allah's circumambulation of the Ka'ba would, in future times, be remembered as "The good old days!" In previous times, even while the beloved Prophet was prostrating, the intestines of a camel would be put on his neck. Finally, Almighty Allah had allowed him to enter the Ka'ba as a triumphant commander.

As the idols were cleared of the Ka'ba, our beloved Prophet read a verse of the Qur'an meaning, *"Truth came, superstition disappeared"*. Then he addressed the Meccans who once had not allowed him to live in his homeland. But Prophet Muhammad, peace and blessings be upon him, was the Prophet of Mercy, and he showed mercy by declaring a general amnesty, even to those who had once victimized him. He also declared that those who stayed at home, or left their weapons and took shelter in the Ka'ba would not be hurt. Thus, the day of the conquest of Mecca was also a day of compassion.

The Removal
of Idols

*I*t was a bright day in Mecca, as if the sun shone into people's hearts, mind, and spirit, illuminating them and banishing the dark days of the past. The Messenger of Allah was cleaning up the remains of the old beliefs of Mecca, removing all the idols both within and outside the Ka'ba. They sent troops around Mecca and removed everything contrary to Islam. The blessed Prophet then commanded Khalid to clear away the Uzza idol. Before he set off, the noble Prophet warned Khalid to destroy the first idol of the three gumwoods in Nahla. Khalid had often faced an enemy, but that was the first time his enemy was a tree. Al-Uzza, which was situated near Nahla, was the most important idol worshipped by the Meccans, so it was housed in a building to protect it, with guards and gatekeepers outside.

Following the tradition at the Ka'ba prior to Islam, Meccans would circumambulate the Uzza. Khalid once saw his father sacrifice some of the best sheep in his flock in front of the Uzza. His father would stay there for a few days to worship the idol. Khalid couldn't help thinking about his father worshipping a tree, offering sacrifices to it and wasting his life believing in it. He was going to destroy al-Uzza and prove to everyone that believing in those idols was a waste of time.

So Khalid set out for Nahla with thirty of his friends. On arrival, he cut down the first idol and destroyed the warehouse in which sacrificed foods for idols were kept. Then he returned to Mecca and went to see the Messenger of Allah, who asked him: "Did you destroy the Uzza?"

Khalid answered: "O Messenger of Allah, as you ordered, I went to Nahla and destroyed al-Uzza." The Messenger of Allah asked one more question: "Did you see anything there?" Khalid replied: "I did not see anything other than what you told me." Allah's Messenger continued: "Then you have not destroyed it. Return to Nahla and destroy the other one." Khalid did not understand what the noble Prophet was trying to say. He returned to al-Uzza and this time he saw a scruffy-looking figure, which he destroyed with his sword, exclaiming: "O al-Uzza! I no longer believe in you." Then he returned, went to the blessed Prophet and told him what he had done. The noble Prophet replied: "Now you have destroyed the Uzza." By destroying al-Uzza, the Messenger of Allah removed the last remnants of the old bad faith of the non-believers who used to worship there. Later on, he spread the word of the Muslim religion by inviting nearby tribes to Islam.

The Battle of Hunayn

Hunayn was a valley located between Mecca and Ta'if. At the noble Prophet's time, the tribes of Hawazin and Thaqif used to live there and, after the conquest of Mecca, they decided to attack the Muslims. When the blessed Prophet heard that, he assembled an army and on arriving in Hunayn, prepared for battle. The Messenger of Allah sent in the cavalry, led by Khalid, ahead of the advancing Muslim army. The soldiers included teenagers who had become Muslim after the conquest of Mecca. The blessed Prophet announced that the victory would be theirs, if they showed patience.

It was before sunrise when the army was ordered to attack, and they began to descend slowly to the

Valley of Hunayn. The Hawazins had already arrived and taken control of the valley roads. They were ready to ambush the army of Islam as they waited to attack. The enemy tribes had experienced soldiers with good fighting skills. The Hawazins wanted to show that their very survival was at stake in this war, so they came to the battlefield with their wives, children, animals and goods.

Khalid's troops were showered with arrows by the Hawazins. As a result of heavy attacks by Hawazin soldiers, hidden on either side of the valley, the army of Muslim soldiers began to retreat. All of a sudden, the campaign strategy began to collapse and the soldiers panicked. However, despite all that, the noble Prophet stood firm. Seeing the blessed Prophet's reaction, the Muslims started to attack again. The Hawazins were surprised by their persistence. They began to flee, leaving behind them everything that they brought to the battlefield. With the battle over, the Muslims fell back to rest.

As usual, Khalid had fought on the front line during the battle and shown great heroism, but he was exhausted and was seriously wounded. While his friends were resting, he was standing still, leaning on his horse. He tried to pull himself together when he saw the beloved Prophet coming towards him. The Messenger of Allah looked at his wounds and prayed to Allah for healing, which encouraged Khalid. The blessed Prophet then ordered the soldiers to follow the enemy soldiers who had fled. Khalid walked through the streets of Ta'if at the head of the army. The Ta'if people had offered refuge to the fleeing Hawazin soldiers, and even closed the castle doors behind them. The Muslim army laid siege to the castle and Khalid requested that the Ta'if people surrender the soldiers they were harboring. When they refused to give up the soldiers to Khalid, he told them that most tribes around them had become Muslim, and he invited them to embrace Islam as well. This offer was not accepted by the Ta'if people. With the refusal of the Ta'if people, the noble Prophet ordered the removal of the siege, as he did not want any bloodshed. After some time, the Ta'if people accepted the religion of Islam voluntarily.

The Expedition to Tabuk

*I*t had been nine years since the migration to Medina and the religion of Islam was spreading rapidly through the Arabian Peninsula. Some merchants from Syria reported that Byzantium was not happy about this situation and were preparing an army to fight against the Muslims. Upon hearing this news, the blessed Prophet started his own preparations for war. Despite the difficulties and hardships, he prepared an army of thirty thousand soldiers, including ten thousand cavalry. Under the scorching heat of the sun, and after a long and tiring journey, they arrived in Tabuk, situated on the road to Syria. There the Islamic army waited for the Byzantine army, but when the Byzantine army did not appear, there was no battle and no bloodshed.

For the duration of the noble Prophet's stay in this place, he was inviting all the local tribes to adopt Islam as their religion. Khalid and his cavalry were sent to King Uqaydir. After a little while, he brought King Uqaydir and his brother into the noble Prophet's presence and he invited them to Islam. However, Uqaydir and his brother didn't accept his invitation, but agreed to pay tax and to live under the blessed Prophet's administration.

Delegation of Najran

en years after the migration to Medina, the Messenger of Allah sent Khalid to Najran, which was situated near to the Yemen. There was a warrior tribe there named the Sons of Harith, and they were victorious in almost every battle. The Messenger of Allah told Khalid to invite them to Islam. So Khalid immediately departed and arrived close to Najran. He invited them to Islam by sending his soldiers all over the city. The Najran people told Khalid they would become Muslim. Thus, the noble Prophet's target was achieved. But Khalid still did not want to leave the place without first checking with the blessed Prophet. He wrote a letter explaining the situation but, in the meantime, while await-ing the noble Prophet's reply, continued to explain the beautiful religion of Islam to the Najran people.

It didn't take very long for Khalid's letter to reach the noble Prophet, and he was pleased with the news that Islam was spreading rapidly in the Arabi-an Peninsula. He replied to Khalid, asking him to return to Medina together with a delegation of Najran people. Khalid immediately did as he was asked and returned to Medina with a delegation party. After showing hospitality to the guests, he brought them to the mosque and, in the presence of the blessed Prophet, the envoys reported that they had become Muslim.

When the Messenger of Allah asked the Najran people the secret of their success in battle and how they defeated their enemies, they replied: "We're try-ing to protect our unity and solidarity. We value jus-tice. We're not cruel to anyone. As a result of this, success comes on its own." After listening carefully, the blessed Prophet said: "What you say is true."

Qualities such as justice, unity and solidarity were conclusive for the Najrans' adoption of Islam. The noble Prophet assigned one of his envoys to the Najrans as a governor, and envoys of the Najrans stayed as guests in Khalid's house for ten days, returning home with gifts given by the beloved Prophet.

Caliph
Abu Bakr

The Messenger of Allah passed away, which threw everyone into great confusion and sadness. Receiving the sad news, Abu Bakr, may Allah be pleased with him, came right away and entered his daughter Aisha's, may Allah be pleased with her, room, where the body of the noble Prophet lay. With no word to anyone, he uncovered the blessed face of the blessed Prophet, bent down and, when he saw that he had, indeed, passed away, kissed his forehead. Then, with a tearful voice, he said "Dearer than my father and my mother, O Messenger of Allah!" Then everybody burst into tears and Abu Bakr tried to calm them down, beginning with Umar ibn al-Khattab.

After the death of the beloved Prophet, some tribes attempted mutiny. When some groups refused to give tax to Caliph Abu Bakr, he set out to do battle with them, because they did not recognize the authority of the state. But, because he was head of state, some people, notably Umar ibn al-Khattab and other Companions of the noble Prophet, did not want Abu Bakr to go into battle himself, because they were afraid that there would be turmoil if something bad happened to him. Thereupon Abu Bakr appointed Khalid commander of the troops. Thus, after a minor set-back, Khalid defeated the rebellious tribe and confirmed the noble Prophet's opinion of him: "Khalid is one of the Swords of Allah against hypocrites and polytheists."

Khalid and Musaylima (the False Prophet)

*D*uring Abu Bakr's caliphate, a liar, whose name was Musaylima, started to claim that he was a prophet. Abu Bakr and Khalid ibn al-Walid were appointed to deal with the threat of Musaylima and his rebellion against Islam. He had the support of people from the Yamama region and they had a strong warrior background. Khalid ibn al-Walid could have difficulty against those groups. Abu Bakr was concerned that Khalid ibn al-Walid might have a problem with these people and warned him in a letter: "Be very careful against the Yamama people. You have never battled against a tribe like them. You have to manage this battle in person." But no matter how strong the tribe fighting for Musaylima proved to be, Khalid had more determination than they. When the battle started, Khalid ibn al-Walid said: "I swear to Allah, I'm not going to end the war without destroying Musaylima." By the end of the war, Khalid ibn al-Walid understood why Abu Bakr had warned him about this enemy force. He admitted: "I have met twenty armies in my time, but I have never encountered such an army of warriors."

During the noble Prophet's lifetime, some people from that tribe visited him. But even though they were Muslim, they started to gather around the liar, called Musaylima.

Indeed, one of the blessed Prophet's friends, named Rafi, may Allah be pleased with him, recounts what happened: "Various Arabian tribes came to visit the Messenger of Allah and, of all of them, the Yamama people were the most cold-hearted."

Before battle engaged, Khalid was meeting with his companions to discuss war tactics when his attention was drawn to the Yamama troops who were walking towards each other with swords, and then turning round and going back. Khalid concluded that the enemy army had fallen out with each other, even though there appeared to be no disorder among the troops. In fact, although they appeared to be drawing swords against each other, they were actually holding their swords aloft in the sunshine to soften them and protect them from shattering in battle.

Finally, the two armies began to fight. One of Musaylima's closest companions was killed in the first encounter but his death, far from crushing their resolve, served only to make them battle more fiercely. In the face of strong attacks from the enemy, it was the Muslims who began to retreat, even as far as the tent of the chief commander, Khalid. Meanwhile, the Muslim flag bearers were being martyred one by one. The first flag bearer to die was the brother of Umar ibn al-Khattab. As his flag fell down to the ground, Umar ibn al-Khattab sensed his death, even though he was nowhere near him. Turning towards Yamama he said, "Zayd, may Allah be pleased with you, I can smell your blood."

Umar was so full of pain at the loss of his brother, but what hurt most was that his younger brother had been martyred before him. He said, "Again, you beat me to it!"

This was because Zayd had become a Muslim before Umar; he had loved the noble Prophet and the truths of the Qur'an before Umar; and now, once again, he had left the world with his wings before Umar.

Following Zayd's martyrdom, one of the blessed Prophet's Companions, Salim, may Allah be pleased with him, took the flag. When he saw the retreat of the Muslims, he dug a hole to protect his position, climbed into it and held aloft the flag. But even that course of action could not protect him from death in that fierce battle. After the martyrdom of Salim, Abu Hudhayfa, may Allah be pleased with him, took the flag, but shortly after he was also martyred. The flag was transferred to Yazd ibn Qays, may Allah be pleased with him, who was one of the lions of the Battle of Badr.

Khalid knew how to stop his soldiers retreating. He began to fight as a soldier on the front lines in order to give them courage. Also, appointing Bara ibn Malik, may Allah be pleased with him, as commander of the cavalry changed the course of the war. Bara gathered his troops, and said to them: "My mother and father be your ransom. While attacking the enemy, fight passionately, as if you are ready to die willingly."

From then on, he started to fight passionately. When the soldiers saw both Bara ibn Malik and Khalid risking their own lives to fight, they advanced again. That attack brought an end to the war. The enemy troops could not resist anymore and the Yamama people had to take refuge in a gated garden. Entering the garden with the help of Abu Dujana, may Allah be pleased with him, the Muslims won the war and Musaylima was killed by Wahshi.

During that battle, the Muslims had suffered many martyrs, most of whom were people who had memorized the whole Qur'an. This made them realize that they had to find new ways of preserving the Qur'an, if they were to protect the Muslim faith for future generations. Some Companions of the noble Prophet had also been injured, including Umm Umara, may Allah be pleased with her, who was a female Companion who joined the war with Abu Bakr's permission. Her aim was to kill the false prophet, Musaylima herself but, when she didn't manage that, she made the prostration of thankfulness for the victory. When she was injured in the battle, the chief commander himself, Khalid ibn al-Walid, looked after her needs in person and called for a doctor to treat her.

Victory soon belonged to Abu Bakr. He first prostrated in thankfulness to Allah and then listened to reports of the progress of the battle brought by the envoy. The people of Medina experienced both joy and sorrow with that war. They were happy that the chaos created by the liar Musaylima was ended, but the cost of a martyr from every home also deeply saddened them.

Khalid against the Sassanids

he Sassanid state rulers had great self-confi-
dence and looked down on the Muslim Arabs.
Despite that, and even though they were fire-
worshippers, the noble Prophet sent an envoy and
invited them to Islam. However, their ruler, Chosroes, felt insulted and tore up the letter. The Messenger of Allah was deeply hurt by Chosroes' rude
behavior and rejection of his invitation. Although
cursing was not something the Messenger of Allah
was prone to, on that occasion he cursed Chosroes,
saying: "O Allah, destroy his property, too." Our
beloved Prophet's cursing was taken as an order by
Khalid ibn al-Walid. If Chosroes tore up the noble

Prophet's letter, then he deserved the destruction of his world. Commanded by Abu Bakr, Khalid ibn al-Walid began to attack the regions under Sassanid rule. The whole Sassanid Empire, thanks to Khalid ibn al-Walid's raids, was razed to the ground.

The Conquest of Himis

hen Khalid ibn al-Walid conquered Himis, it was a popular victory with the people there, most of whom were non-Muslims. Under the Byzantines, they had been forced to pay unfair taxes, so they willingly paid the poll tax, levied on non-Muslims under Islamic administration, in return for services provided, particularly for protection. At first, everything was fine. However, Khalid was a conquest-hungry soldier and when he decided to engage the Byzantine Emperor's army, he withdrew his soldiers from Himis and sent them to Yarmuk. Thus, Himis was deprived of their public security force.

As a result, Khalid returned the taxes he had taken from the Himis people and told them: "Because we are busy with the Battle of Yarmuk, we are unable to help you. As we won't be able to protect you, it is your responsibility to ensure your own safety."

Khalid's method of justice merely bewildered the Himis people. They sent a delegation to Khalid and said: "Your decision upset us. No matter what happens, we want to stay under your protection. The Byzantine army will not be able to take over here again."

The Jews living in Himis were also contented with Khalid's justice. They stood up and said: "We swear on the Old Testament that the Byzantines will have to destroy us first if they want Himis." When they left Khalid's presence, they closed the city gates and took control of the city's security.

Other neighboring non-Muslim cities also acted in the same way, saying: "If the Byzantine army wins the battle against Khalid's army, then we will return to the old corrupt order. Even if only one Muslim soldier remains alive, we will stay true to our word given to Khalid.

Khalid ibn al-Walid's military genius had a unique place in history. With only a small army, he defeated an entire Byzantine army. The Himis people celebrated his victory with a fanfare of trumpets.

Khalid in the Suwa Desert

halid ibn al-Walid had taken his conquering army into Iraq, whereas Caliph Abu Bakr was more interested in Syrian conquests. He sent a letter to Khalid telling him: "I appoint you as the commander of the army. Go at once to Damascus and when you arrive there, you will get another letter. I want you to follow the instructions in the letter exactly."

Having read the letter, Khalid set off for Damascus. Once there, the Caliph's second letter containing his orders was delivered to him. His instructions were to make a long and arduous journey through the desert, which could well be life-threatening. But

Khalid ibn al-Walid was a highly disciplined soldier and, as far as he was concerned, orders are to be obeyed at all costs. As soon as he got the order, he enlisted the help of a guide, called Rafi, may Allah be pleased with him, to help him find his way through the desert. When Rafi realized the enormity of the task, he said: "You can't cross the desert with these loaded horses; it's too long a journey and the route is difficult. In addition, it's almost impossible to find water. Even with a very strong horse, it would take five days to complete the journey. If you insist on crossing this desert, you will be putting your soldiers' lives at risk." But Khalid's mind was made up; he must cross that desert. So he replied: "These are my orders from Caliph Abu Bakr himself. Make the necessary arrangements."

Rafi was surprised by Khalid's determination, and began to make the following plans: "So we need to take lots of water with us. Also, we need to find twenty large-bodied camels." Khalid ibn al-Walid supplied what he requested. Then he said: "Now we can load our goods and set off."

When preparations were complete, the caravan set off on its journey, but soon ran into trouble. By noon, the soldiers were so thirsty they could hardly stand, and by the end of the day, they had run out of water. When Khalid saw that his soldiers' lives were at risk, he told Rafi: "It's not possible to continue on this route. We have to find water." Rafi replied: "Don't be alarmed. There must be water somewhere. Pray that I remember where to find it."

Rafi tried to remember. If he remembered correctly, there was a tree which looked like a crouching human figure, and water flowed by that tree. He asked the soldiers: "Have you seen a tree which looks like a crouching human figure?" It was obvious from their response that the soldiers hadn't seen the tree. Rafi was upset and told them, "Then we are at risk. We have to find that tree if we are to survive. Please look around carefully."

The soldiers continued to search for the tree and eventually found it. When they saw the tree all the soldiers, and Rafi, too, praised Allah by saying the *takbir* (Allahu Akbar). When they dug at the bottom of the tree, they saw a bubbling spring of water. First, they drank thirstily and filled their canteens and pots, and then they continued their journey.

It was thanks to the sharp eyes and powerful memory of Rafi that the soldiers were able to cross the Suwa Desert without loss of life. Rafi had only once before been to that place, as a child with his father, yet even with the passing of many years, he had not forgotten it.

Khalid ibn al-Walid ﷺ

The Battle
of Yarmuk

halid ibn al-Walid engaged in battle with
the Byzantine Emperor Heraclius in the
Battle of Yarmuk. When Khalid saw the
massive army of the Emperor Heraclius, he devised
a new tactic for the battle. It would be dangerous to
show the full strength of his army immediately, so
he separated his soldiers into small units and troops
joined the army at intervals. That tactic dampened
the morale of the Byzantine army.

Thanks to Khalid ibn al-Walid's military genius,
his army won the battle and Syria came under Muslim control. Nor was it only Muslims who celebrated their victory. Non-Muslims, too, being sick of the

Byzantine Emperor's administration, celebrated that victory with a fanfare of trumpets.

It was at the Battle of Yarmuk that Khalid ibn al-Walid included Muslim women in the war effort. One woman fighting under his command, Asma bint Yazd, may Allah be pleased with her, killed nine enemy soldiers with a tent pole during that war. She wasn't just known for her courage in the battlefield. She was brave enough to ask difficult questions of the noble Prophet to gain a better understanding of Islam. Once, she asked the blessed Prophet the following question: "Dearer than my father and my mother, O Messenger of Allah! I was sent as an ambassador by women. Allah sent you as a Prophet for all men and women. As women, we believe in you and Allah. But we are made to stay at home, raising our children and serving our husbands. You men, on the other hand, perform Friday prayer, go to mosques and worship, visit sick people, make the funeral prayer, and go on pilgrimage. More importantly, you are considered better than us at fighting in the cause of Allah and defending our faith. And, while you set off to serve Allah in this way, we women remain behind to protect your goods, mend your clothes and feed your children. Why can we not be given the same validation and responsibilities as you men?

The Messenger of Allah was pleased with her question. He asked his followers: "Have you heard any better question asked by a woman about our religion?" His followers replied: "O Messenger of Allah! We've never heard such beautiful sentiments."

Then the beloved Prophet instructed her: "O lady! Listen to and remember what I say to you and explain it to other women. If a woman gets on well with her husband and pleases him, it is equal to all those virtues found in men."

Relieved
of Duty

hen Umar ibn al-Khattab arrived in Syria, he reviewed the goods and assets of public officials with Bilal al-Habashi, may Allah be pleased with him. First of all he visited Abu Ubayda's, may Allah be pleased with him, house and carried out an inspection. Then he and Bilal went on to Khalid's house, announced themselves and were invited in. Khalid was busy with his arrow. Umar noticed a crate in the house and opened it for examination. It contained armor made of iron.

Khalid was angry about the search and complained: "Look! I swear by Allah that if I had not found faith in Allah and Islam, you would have no jurisdiction over me."

Whenever Khalid entered battle, the Muslim army, with Allah's help, would always win, and it was in part for this reason that most people trusted him. The resulting achievements were seen to be due to his military genius. It wasn't wrong to trust Khalid, but to give him too much credit was unwise, and that did not escape the attention of Umar ibn al-Khattab. People must be reminded of the fact that all the battles were won with the help of Allah. Umar ibn al-Khattab had to drive that point home, so he took command of the army away from Khalid to reveal that misconception. Khalid ibn al-Walid was an obedient person. When he found out that he was relieved from his command, he called out: "The Chief of Believers appointed me Commander of Damascus. I have conquered Syria and made peace there. After this, someone else took over my duties." Hearing this, one of those present said: "O Khalid, this is a test (*fitna*) for you. Be patient." Khalid replied: "As long as Umar ibn al-Khattab is alive, there cannot be a test."

Before long, Umar ibn al-Khattab heard what Khalid was saying, and he declared: "It is not Khalid but Allah who helped Islam and enabled the

Muslims to be victorious. Khalid is merely an intermediary and that is why I relieved him of his duty. Such a wise insight of Umar ibn al-Khattab, proved what the blessed Prophet had said about him: "Allah reveals the truth on Umar's tongue and heart." The noble Prophet's words were proof that Umar ibn al-Khattab was a straightforward person who made the right decisions.

The Messenger of Allah also said this about Umar ibn al-Khattab: "In previous times, Allah picked out certain people in a community and gave them His blessing through these people. There are people like that in my Community (*Ummah*) also. Umar is one of them."

Umar ibn al-Khattab sent a letter to Khalid ibn al-Walid in which he wrote: "I did not relieve you from your duty out of anger or to betray you. My reason was that it is Allah who should receive the glory, and I wanted people to understand this."

Abu Ubayda ibn Jarrah was appointed to take the place of Khalid. Abu Ubayda was one of ten people who, while still living, was promised a place in Paradise.

Abu Ubayda was chosen because he could explain the beautiful religion of Islam to people living in conquered places. Khalid and Abu Ubayda used to love and respect each other. On one occasion, these two commanders, who conquered Damascus, were about to start performing the prayer when Abu Ubayda said to Khalid: "You lead the prayer; you're worthy of this because you came here to help me." But Khalid replied: "The Messenger of Allah said that I can't take priority over you in leading the prayer."

Khalid returned to Medina after his dismissal and from there traveled to Mecca to perform his minor pilgrimage. Later on, he returned to Humus and spent the rest of his life there.

His Death

Khalid ibn al-Walid died in a village in the city of Humus in Syria. When he passed away, women gathered and began to cry. People asked Umar ibn al-Khattab: "Please stop these women crying." This was because it was not considered appropriate for Muslims to lose control and cry out loud when mourning a dead person. However, Umar advised them: "Let these women cry for Khalid. Unless they pour soil on their heads and scream and shout, shedding tears is not objectionable."

While washing the dead body of Khalid, they came across the scars in many parts of his body. Before his death, Khalid had appointed Umar as his guardian, and left nothing other than his horses, weapons and a maid.

Abu Bakr said about Khalid: "We shall never see the like of Khalid again."

The blessed Prophet also praised Khalid with these words: "Khalid ibn al-Walid is such a great servant of Allah; he is one of the Swords of Allah."

Khalid ibn al-Walid was also kind to his soldiers while he ruled them with authority. He would always tell his soldiers: "Patience is the highest virtue; defeat is feebleness; victory is only won by patience."